美国权利法案

How We Organize Ourselves | Non-Fiction Series

Copyright © 2022 by Level Learning, INC. and Washington Yu Ying PCS™
Original and Edited Text Copyright © 2022 by Washington Yu Ying PCS™

All rights reserved. No part of this book in whole or part may be reproduced without written permission from the publisher.

Published by Level Learning, INC.

Content Contributors:
Washington Yu Ying PCS™ - Aini Fang, Pearl Zao He You
Level Learning - Jingyao Qi

Illustrations by: Josh Taira

Leveling classification based on Level Learning standard. For full description, visit www.levellearning.com

ISBN 978-1-64040-118-1
Simplified Chinese Edition

About Level Learning:
Level Learning provides a literacy focused curriculum specifically designed for K-12 Chinese as a Second Language classrooms. Our program offers 20 levels of specific and detailed objectives, leveled texts and passages, mastery-based online assessment, and analytics to enable data-driven instruction. Level Learning reading curriculum for both literature and informational text emphasize grammar and comprehension skills to help teachers develop confident and independent Chinese language readers. The non-fiction series of books are specifically designed to support our informational text course based on multiple national standards. To learn more about our entire offering, visit www.levellearning.com.

About Washington Yu Ying PCS™:
Washington Yu Ying PCS is a Mandarin English dual language immersion International Baccalaureate (IB) World school. Yu Ying's mission is to inspire and prepare young people to create a better world by challenging them to reach their full potential in a nurturing Chinese/English educational environment. Yu Ying's comprehensive IB, dual immersion curriculum equips students with global competencies for success in the real world. As a leader in immersion education, Yu Ying is determined to advance Chinese language programs and global citizenry education by helping other schools create and strengthen their Chinese programs. For more information, email: products@washingtonyuying.org

什么是美国权利法案？美国宪法有27条修正案。美国权利法案是美国宪法的前10条修正案。

JAMES MADISON
詹姆士·麦迪逊

1789年，美国国会一共提出了12条修正案。1791年12月15日，这12条修正案中的10条被通过了。这10条修正案就是美国权利法案。

美国权利法案以保护公民权利为主。其中的第一条和第四条尤其和人们的生活息息相关。

美国权利法案第一条修正案：人们的宗教和言论自由受到保护。

这一条修正案的意思是：人们有权利选择或改变自己的宗教信仰，这就是宗教自由。有的人信佛教、有的人信基督教、也有的人信伊斯兰教等。当然，你也可以选择没有宗教信仰。

人们也可以自由地说出自己的想法，这就是言论自由。但是，你的言论不能给其他人造成伤害。比如说，在没有火灾的时候，如果你大叫"着火啦，快逃啊！"这可能会引起恐慌，造成伤害。这就不是言论自由的一部分了。

美国权利法案第四条修正案：人们的人身和财产不可以受到没有理由的搜查。

在1791年权利法案被通过的时候，这条修正案里的人身和财产还只是代表一个人的身体、房子、车子等。但是，随着科学技术的发展，人们在网络上创造了另一个世界。每天都有成千上万人把自己的个人信息或照片放在网络上，同时，这些信息也被以各种各样的方式传播或使用着。这样算是违法吗？网络信息是不是应该算作人身财产而受到保护呢？

什么是合法？什么是违法？法官们需要根据权利法案第四条，也根据不同的情况做出判断。

如果你有机会来首都华盛顿旅游，一定要去参观一下美国国家档案馆。在那里展示着美国权利法案的原稿哦！

Glossary

	Pinyin	English Definition
权利法案	quán lì fǎ àn	Bill of Rights
宪法	xiàn fǎ	constitution
修正案	xiū zhèng àn	amendment
以……为主	yǐ……wéi zhǔ	as main focus
保护	bǎo hù	to protect
公民权利	gōng mín quán lì	civil rights
尤其	yóu qí	especially
息息相关	xī xī xiāng guān	closely related
宗教	zōng jiào	religious
言论	yán lùn	speech
自由	zì yóu	freedom
受到	shòu dào	to receive
宗教信仰	zōng jiào xìn yǎng	religious belief
佛教	fó jiào	Buddhism
基督教	jī dū jiào	Christianity

	Pinyin	English Definition
伊斯兰教	yī sī lán jiào	Islam
当然	dāng rán	certainly
比如	bǐ rú	such as
引起	yǐn qǐ	to cause
恐慌	kǒng huāng	panic
造成	zào chéng	to cause
财产	cái chǎn	property
理由	lǐ yóu	reason
搜查	sōu chá	to search
代表	dài biǎo	to represent
网络	wǎng luò	Internet
信息	xìn xī	information
传播	chuán bō	to spread
违法	wéi fǎ	to break the law
合法	hé fǎ	lawful, legal

Glossary

	Pinyin	English Definition
根据	gēn jù	according to
判断	pàn duàn	judgement
首都	shǒu dū	capital
参观	cān guān	to visit
国家档案馆	guó jiā dàng àn guǎn	National Archives
原稿	yuán gǎo	manuscript, original copy

www.ingramcontent.com/pod-product-compliance
Lightning Source LLC
Chambersburg PA
CBHW041221070526
44584CB00001B/37